Cryptocurrency Investing For Beginner's without the Guesswork

How to Make Money with Cryptocurrency Easily Explained

© **Copyright 2017 by Alex McCandles** - All rights reserved.

This document is geared towards providing exact and reliable information in regards to the topic and issue covered. The publication is sold with the idea that the publisher is not required to render accounting, officially permitted, or otherwise, qualified services. If advice is necessary, legal or professional, a practiced individual in the profession should be ordered.

- From a Declaration of Principles which was accepted and approved equally by a Committee of the American Bar Association and a Committee of Publishers and Associations.

In no way is it legal to reproduce, duplicate, or transmit any part of this document in either electronic means or in printed format. Recording of this publication is strictly prohibited and any storage of this document is not allowed unless with written permission from the publisher. All rights reserved.

The information provided herein is stated to be truthful and consistent, in that any liability, in terms of inattention or otherwise, by any usage or abuse of any policies, processes, or directions contained within is the solitary and utter responsibility of the recipient reader. Under no circumstances will any legal responsibility or blame be held against the publisher for any reparation, damages, or monetary loss due to the information herein, either directly or indirectly.

Respective authors own all copyrights not held by the publisher.

The information herein is offered for informational purposes solely, and is universal as so. The presentation of the information is without contract or any type of guarantee assurance.

The trademarks that are used are without any consent, and the publication of the trademark is without permission or backing by the trademark owner. All trademarks and brands within this book are for clarifying purposes only and are the owned by the owners themselves, not affiliated with this document.

Table of Contents

Chapter 1 - Currency vs. Money............8

Chapter 2 - Shakiness Of Fiat Paper Money...................... 12

Chapter 3 - Benefits of Cryptocurrency 17

Chapter 4 - Best Cryptocurrencies 22

Chapter 5 - All About Bitcoins 28

Chapter 6 - Bitcoin Investing Strategies 52

Chapter 7 - All About Ethereum 55

Chapter 8 - Litecoin 101...................... 69

Chapter 9 - Cryptocurrency Wallets.... 90

Chapter 10 - How to Invest in Cryptocurrencies.................................98

Chapter 11 - Tips and Tricks for Investing 107

Chapter 12 - Cryptocurrency Exchanges 119

Conclusion 136

Introduction

I would like to thank you for purchasing the book " Cryptocurrency Investing For Beginners Without The Guesswork- How To Make Money With Cryptocurrency Easily Explained."

The system that governs the monetary system, the way it works with all the middlemen and brokers, has stayed relatively the same for centuries now. However, there is a better alternative to it now, and this puts us on the brink of a revolution that can potentially reshape the economies of our world. At the heart of this change lie cryptocurrencies, a technology with immense potential. Cryptocurrencies do away with the elites and the gatekeepers. Unlike the fiat currencies we use, cryptocurrencies are based on a peer-to-peer network, they don't have a nationality and they are digitized and quite democratic. The invention of cryptocurrencies has opened up the world economic system to anyone who has access to a computer, and the possibilities of their usage are numerous. From the Silicon Valley to the streets of Beijing, this book will provide you with information about this futuristic currency.

The Bitcoin was invented back in 2008, and there's been no turning back since then. Cryptocurrencies have become commonplace, and it is essential to learn about it because this technology is here to stay. Cryptocurrencies are easier to transact with, safer, and cheaper when compared to credit cards or fiat currencies. In this book, you will learn about cryptocurrency, why it is better than money, the different advantages it offers, about fractional reserve banking, the pros and cons of the Federal Reserve, about Bitcoins, the various benefits they offer, learn investing strategies and everything else a beginner needs to know before buying Bitcoins. So, why don't we get started?

Chapter 1 - Currency vs. Money

Currency and money aren't synonyms though they are used synonymously. If you look the meanings of these words up in a thesaurus, they will indeed be listed as a synonym. However, their economic functioning is different. In this chapter, you will understand the difference between these two so that you can preserve your wealth.

Currency

For most, currency or fiat currency refers to the hard earned cash or cash in hand. It includes dollars, pounds, euros, yen, and all other types of physical currency notes that you can keep in your wallet. The primary medium of economic exchange in a country is currency, and it could be in the form of paper or coins. Currency was made of precious metals, and these materials were quite difficult to transport. The idea was to create a kind of movable currency that would serve the same purpose and was backed up by precious metals. For instance, banknotes are usually backed by precious metals like gold or silver. These banknotes can be exchanged for their legal tender anytime. Legal tender refers to the precious metals that back such notes. The US silver certificates can be exchanged for their worth in silver. The US adopted the gold standard in 1879, and since then the currency is backed by certain precious metals that lend credibility to the issuing government. People accepted this currency system since they knew their wealth was secured by the precious metals backing it.

Gold standard

The gold standard was done away with in 1993 by the US Congress and President Roosevelt. This disabled US citizens from demanding the payment of their currency in gold. The public had to transfer all their gold coin, bullion and gold certificates to the Federal Reserve at a predetermined price. The Federal government has the power to regulate the money in circulation since they were controlling all the gold. During this period, inflation was created for stimulating the economy. It is ironic that the system of the gold standard was done away with for building public confidence in the economic system. In 1971, President Nixon declared the gold standard obsolete. US citizens were then introduced to the concept of fiat currency that isn't backed by any precious metals and instead depends on the confidence of people in the government.

Money

Money is referred to as commodity money, and the commodity could be anything ranging from seashells to stones. This is a medium of exchange that is used for buying and selling goods and services, and for the repayment of debt as well. Precious metals are finite, but fiat currency is capable of being printed according to the government's desires. Gold is absolute, whereas fiat currencies aren't. These precious metals cannot be created nor destroyed, only transformed and they can exist forever. You cannot apply the same concept to the paper money you carry with you. Fiat currencies are inherently transient, and their value depends on the rise and fall of their nations.

Chapter 2 - Shakiness Of Fiat Paper Money

Modern currencies like the dollar, euro, yen, pound, and so on are all forms of fiat currency. Fiat currency is also referred to as artificial currency. A unit of fiat currency is worth its purchasing power, and there is no set standard for measuring its value. Fiat currency is quite shaky and here are the disadvantages of fiat currencies.

Money and its value

If you have seen the movie "The Matrix," then you can recollect a scene in which Neo has a conversation with a particularly gifted child who can bend spoons by using the power of his mind. In this scene, the child tells Neo that instead of concentrating on bending the spoon, one must simply understand it. The truth is, there is no spoon, and it is your mind that you have to bend. Similarly, abstraction and abstracts are different concepts altogether. Abstractions are made use of for describing the world whereas an abstract is the mental representation of a concept that can only be described in relativity like law or justice. Abstracts are ideas that just exist in the human mind. For instance, law talks about justice, but an arbitrary law will still be a law even if it is unjust. Making a declaration that a stone is a seafaring vessel doesn't grant the stone the power to float. The system of fiat money is based on a similarly absurd concept. Money and its value are abstractions and an abstract respectively. Fiat money has no value on its own accord.

Coercion

This is a basic characteristic of all fiat currencies. Most wouldn't accept it unless they are forced to. For instance, the gold standard in was replaced by using legal force in the United States. US citizens were forced to accept the Federal Reserve notes instead of the gold certificates under the threat of incurring a penalty and/or imprisonment. The scheme of fiat currencies is immoral since the primary factor responsible for their acceptance is coercion. The power of controlling this currency lies in the hands of few, and they are capable of altering the availability, its quantum, and its distribution in the economy.

Rent seeking

Fiat currency system is designed for extracting rent by the forceful conduct of commerce in the system of existing fiat currency. The ability to trade is as natural as any other human rights like the right to life and liberty. In a marketplace that is formed on voluntary arrangements, there shouldn't be any middlemen trying to extract economic rent for their said permission to engage in trade and commerce.

Central planning

Fiat currency is based on coercive and not voluntary relationships. Only the central government or any such authority has the monopoly over these currencies. Economic planning isn't democratic. The human society indeed isn't blessed with individuals who are infallible for taking sound economic and financial decisions. A decision taken by a small population affects everyone else.

Instability

Central planners have the power to decide the quantum of fiat currency that should be in circulation. It is impossible to get the right figure, and any discrepancies in this can have horrible repercussions on the rest of the economy. It leads to instability in prices and creates artificial depression. Price stability cannot be achieved by following this system. Instability and volatility go hand in hand. Fiat currencies are bound to come untethered after a while. Identifying the wrong quantity can lead to a credit boom, depression, recession, and even the collapse of the economy. Fiat currencies merely magnify the volatility of an economy.

Redistribution and concentration of wealth

An increase in the currency in an economy leads to the distortion of its purchasing power and an unfair redistribution of wealth, thereby efficiently stealing wealth from a significant chunk of society. Redistribution of wealth and further uneven distribution of it cannot do the economy any good.

Moral hazards

The concentration of power in the hands of a few individuals, more often than not, leads to corruption. Fiat currencies are prone to all forms of moral hazards, and the individuals who are controlling its production can go wrong as well. All in all, there are plenty of disadvantages of the present currency system that we are making use of.

Chapter 3 - Benefits of Cryptocurrency

The simplicity of cryptocurrencies is its main strength. The elimination of middlemen and other regulatory authorities along with the ease of transactions make cryptocurrencies a great option. In the initial phase, it might have seemed scary just like credit cards did during their initial days. You probably will have heard of different cryptocurrencies like Bitcoins or Ether. These cryptocurrencies make use of the ingenious blockchain technology that makes them secure. In this chapter, let us take a look at all the different advantages this currency offers to its users.

No scams
Cryptocurrencies cannot be forged because of their digitized nature. Not just that but cryptocurrencies eliminate the scope of a transaction being arbitrarily reversed by a sender. Credit cards create the possibility of a

chargeback, and this is done away with this digitized currency.

Instant settlements

If you want to purchase real property, then regardless of whether you like it or not, there will be a few third parties like lawyers, notaries or brokers involved in it along with delays and fee payment. Cryptocurrencies are similar to a large database of property rights. The cryptocurrency contracts are designed in a manner that eliminates the involvement of third parties, and they can be enforced without the approval or third parties and any reference to other external facts. The time taken for the settlement of a cryptocurrency contract is far less than that required for a regular contract or agreement.

Lower fees

No transaction fee is payable on cryptocurrency exchange since all the miners are compensated for by the network itself. Even though there isn't a transaction fee, most users make use of third-party services for the creation and the maintenance of their cryptocurrency wallets.

Identity theft

Whenever you give a vendor or a merchant your credit card, you are automatically giving them access to your credit line regardless of the amount involved in the transaction. Credit cards function on a pull basis- as soon as the vendor has initiated a payment; the concerned amount is automatically pulled from your account. All cryptocurrencies make use of a push mechanism. The holder of the cryptocurrency needs to send the exact amount to the merchant, and only the holder can authorize such a transaction.

Ease of access

More than 2.2 billion people all over the globe have access to the Internet and smartphone, but not everyone has access to the traditional exchanges. Cryptocurrency is best suited for such people, and there are plenty of mobile-based services that help in the transfer of cryptocurrencies.

Decentralization

A vast network of computers spread all over the world make use of the blockchain technology for transacting in cryptocurrencies and maintenance of a database of transactions. A single regulatory authority like the government or central banks doesn't control cryptocurrency. It forms a collaborating power instead of a controlling one.

Universal recognition

A huge network of computers all over the world makes use of Blockchain technology for managing the Bitcoin database and the transactions. A network manages Bitcoin, and a single authority does not control it. Decentralization in here would signify that the system will operate on a peer-to-peer basis or a user-to-user basis. This helps to form a collaborative space instead of a controlling authority.

Universal recognition

There are no interest or exchange rates that control cryptocurrencies, and there are no transaction costs or charges levied on them. So, a user can make international transactions without incurring any additional charges. This saves time, effort and money while conducting a transaction. There is no system of electronic cash that you can make use of which isn't owned by a third party. For instance, in the case of PayPal, if the company is of the opinion that a particular account is being misused then they have the power to freeze all activity and the account itself without consulting the user. When you make use of cryptocurrency, you are the only one with access. Only a user with a private key can access his or her account, and no one else can do that.

When made use of in the proper manner, the potential of cryptocurrency is unparalleled, and no other currency can compete with it.

Chapter 4 - Best Cryptocurrencies

The world of cryptocurrency is growing at a rapid pace, and since its conception, Bitcoin has managed to outperform other investments like gold, stocks, or even the real estate segment. Plenty of new cryptocurrencies have come into existence, and only a handful of these have features that make them different from the rest. These cryptocurrencies are the true outliers - the ones with the power to change or transform the financial and economic sector. In this chapter, you will learn about the best cryptocurrencies that you can invest in. The following cryptocurrencies haven't been mentioned in any particular order, and they all make potentially good investments.

Ethereum

This indeed is a real outlier. The Ethereum platform provides a framework for executing smart contracts that run on a decentralized network. The team managing Ethereum is full of digital wizards who are good at what they do. Apart from the team, the degree of adoption that ether enjoys is quite phenomenal as well. A developer can make use of Ethereum for running Dapps (distributed applications), and it is a peer-to-peer network. These computer programs could be made up of anything, and the network has been optimized to carry out rules that will help in the execution of standards mechanically when a couple of conditions have been met, like a contract for instance.

Ethereum makes use of its very own decentralized public blockchain mechanism for storing data in a cryptographical manner, executes it, and even protects these contracts. Every computer on this network will download a very small virtual machine that is made use of for syncing this to the Ethereum blockchain and is available for the execution of different contracts. This diverse network of different computers provides convenience, security, reliability and the computing prowess that you will need for the implementation of particular arrangements. This network isn't free or even private, so developers just make use of it for obtaining consensus on outcomes and when their data is publicly available. It doesn't operate the way a digital currency or payment system would and instead, it aims to provide "fuel" that will help in the functioning of the Dapps or decentralized applications on the network. This might sound a little complicated, but it isn't. Think of this as a decentralized online notebook and for deleting, posting, or modifying a note; you will be required to pay a transaction fee in the form of Ether to make the necessary changes.

Factom

This is a brilliant cryptocurrency, and it used to be referred to as "notary chain." It facilitates companies to create their immutable databases. The information is stored within its own blockchain and then a data hash is generated. The team behind Factom is working on adding that hash into other cryptocurrencies and a bigger blockchain for better protection. In fact, Factom received a major contract with 20 smart cities in

China and is working with other countries for the creation of mutation-free databases. The market cap of this cryptocurrency is well beyond $10,500,000 at the moment. A really good thing about Factom is that it is being adopted quite quickly by the masses.

MaidSafe

This has been around for over ten years, and it is a decentralized database as well. By using MaidSafe, you are free to encrypt your data and then upload the same onto a decentralized server instead of storing it all on your computer. No one is allowed to access your data without your authorization and therefore it is secure. Also, it doesn't take up any extra space. The decentralized database makes it secure for a whistleblower to share information without fearing the government or any other regulatory authority who might censor them.

Bitcoin

One of the most popular cryptocurrencies today is Bitcoin. Over the last couple of years, this currency has certainly proved its mettle. A Bitcoin is worth more than an ounce of gold at present. The Bitcoin network is quite effective while conducting transactions and provides complete anonymity to the users. It makes use of the blockchain technology for securing the transactions. You will learn more about Bitcoins in the coming chapters.

Litecoin

Charles Lee, a former Google engineer, unveiled Litecoin. Litecoin was introduced as the "silver" to the "gold" of Bitcoin. Lee had come up with the idea of Litecoin to fix the problems that Bitcoins posed. Litecoin doesn't get issued by a government like other currencies. The government has singularly been the entity throughout the history that has been responsible for minting money. The Federal Reserve doesn't regulate Litecoins, and they aren't minted by a press at the Bureau of Engraving and Printing. A complicated process referred to as mining instead creates Litecoins. This process comprises the processing and verification of several Litecoin transactions. Unlike fiat currency, there is a cap on the number of Litecoins present. There can be no more than 84 million Litecoins in circulation. A block is generated on the Litecoin network in every 2.5 minutes. The block is made up of ledger entries of Litecoin transactions that take place around the world. This is where a Litecoin derives its value. The block of transactions is verified by using mining software and is visible to any miner who wishes to see it. Once a block is verified, the next block will enter the chain, and this would contain the record of all the Litecoin transactions ever transacted.

Chapter 5 - All About Bitcoins

In this chapter, you will learn about the basics of Bitcoins.

Origin of Bitcoin

Satoshi Nakamoto is credited with the creation of Bitcoins, and his motivation for creating Bitcoins was to provide a very simple solution to all the different problems that the usual monetary system suffers from. In a world that's dominated by the unstable fiat currencies, Bitcoin came as a breath of fresh air. The central bank and other regulatory authorities are responsible for the devaluation of currency for making all the goods and services offered in the market seem cheaper in the international market. The constant price fluctuations in fiat currency are commonplace, and it has forced the common public to experience the brunt of fiscal deficits and unnecessary inflations within the economy. This lead to the creation of a decentralized currency and thus the Bitcoin was conceptualized. Bitcoin places the control of the financial system in the hands of the public and its users instead of a regulatory body.

An open source code was used for creating Bitcoins, and this means anyone is capable of accessing this platform, of making necessary improvements and building platforms in addition to the existing ones. Modern banking systems can incorporate blockchain technology that forms the basis of Bitcoins into their regular banking system. Bitcoin has great potential because it managed to disrupt the entire fiat currency system that's state-approved and make it user-friendly and more accessible to the general public, thereby creating a great alternative to the traditional fiscal system.

Bitcoins are revolutionary, even more so when there is a constant interaction between the technology and financial aspects of the world. Nakamoto managed to develop a system that gets rid of all middlemen like brokers and even the governmental agencies for its functioning. The Bitcoin ecosystem comprises only of its users. Therefore, if there weren't any users, then there wouldn't be any Bitcoins in existence. The greater the number of users is the more effective this network will be. This system not only depends on its users, but it belongs to them as well. Bitcoin financial network is based on the concept of peer-to-peer sharing wherein a transaction takes place between two users without the involvement of middlemen at any given point of time. Bitcoin is an elegant yet simple concept. For instance, if X has to transfer certain Bitcoins to Y, then the only ones involved in the transaction are X and Y. This monetary system is easily accessible to all the users, and anyone can set their business up and make this the choice of payment.

Brief history of Bitcoins

The title of the paper published by Satoshi Nakamoto that led to the creation of Bitcoin was "Bitcoin: A Peer-to-Peer Electronic Cash System." In this paper, the different ways in which this peer-to-peer system can be used for the generation of financial transactions by eliminating the need for middlemen was explained in great details. In the year 2009, the Bitcoin network came into existence. The first open source code client of the Bitcoin was released, and Bitcoins were issued. Nakamoto generated the first block of Bitcoins and he received 50 Bitcoins for doing this. The first Bitcoin transaction that took place was between Hal Finney and Nakamoto when Finney downloaded the Bitcoin client, and he received 10 Bitcoins for doing the same.

By 2011, several companies like WikiLeaks started accepting Bitcoin donations and the new financial regime was gaining in its popularity, and then there was no turning back. Several viral videos were published about Bitcoins, and this was when Vitalik Buterin co-founded the first magazine about Bitcoins. The Bitcoin Foundation was incorporated for promoting the foray of Bitcoins around the world through regulation, promotion, and the protection of the Bitcoin protocol.

The Bitcoin Foundation was founded by Gavin Andersen, Jon Matonis, Charlie

Shrem, Peter Vsessened and Patrick Murck. The transactional logs of Bitcoin referred to as the blockchain was split into two separate chains that operated on different rules regarding the processing and acceptance of the transactions. These two networks were somehow operating simultaneously for about 6 hours, and each had a different version of the transactional history. This made the developers suspend all the transactions. This resulted in a huge sell-off, and normal operations were restored, and most of the network had to be downgraded. 2013 was the year when Bitcoins were integrated into the economies of several countries. Bitcoin reached a new high in 2017. Well, the value of one Bitcoin is more than that of an ounce of gold. As on 1st May, one Bitcoin was valued at US$1400.

What is a Bitcoin?
Bitcoin is an electronic form of currency that is arranged in a lengthy code that is easily circulated on the Internet and is governed by a diverse body of millions of users who are known as miners. Bitcoin is a virtual currency that is self-contained for its value. It is a type of

cryptocurrency; therefore, it eliminates the need to depend on a bank for storing all this money for transacting or safekeeping. Once you have its ownership, it is similar to holding gold coins or bullion that can be made further use of for acquiring other things. People usually hold onto these Bitcoins in the hope that their value will increase. Well, they aren't wrong in thinking this. Within no time, cryptocurrencies have become more expensive than gold.

Bitcoins are traded from wallet to another. This is a private database capable of being stored on a hard drive or the cloud as well. Bitcoins are certainly quite secure and cannot be forged like regular fiat currency. The computational effort that would be necessary for forging a single Bitcoin renders the process worthless.

Just like regular currency, the price of a Bitcoin keeps fluctuating as well. You can check the price of this cryptocurrency on different websites like Coindesk.com. Only a finite number of coins can exist and this makes them all the more valuable. Since the demand for the coins keeps increasing without a corresponding increase in the supply, Bitcoins are quite precious. The combined value of all the Bitcoins at present is around $2 billion. About 21 million Bitcoins have been mined up to today's date. This financial system is decentralized in nature, so there is no room for the intervention by a regulatory authority like governments, banks, or other middlemen for its safekeeping. Miners are scatted all across the glove, and they have devoted computers whose sole purpose is to monitor the transactions on the network. The transactional logs are public information, and they are all cross-referenced by millions of miners, thereby making sure that there is no scope for discrepancies to creep into this network. A miner is rewarded Bitcoins for every block of data that they mine.

Who created it?

A software developer named Satoshi Nakamoto proposed the idea of Bitcoin. It is an electronic payment system based on several mathematical equations. The basic idea was to create a type of currency that isn't dependent on a central authority while capable of being transformed into an electronic form for quick and cheap execution of transactions.

Who prints these Bitcoins?

No one is authorized to print them, and they cannot be printed in a physical form. Since they are present in digitized format, it eliminates the need for a physical copy. Banks can produce as many notes as they want with the prior approval of the government for covering national debt and this, in turn, leads to the devaluation of the currency. Since Bitcoins are created digitally, people can join the network quite easily. A distributed network is made use of for mining Bitcoins, and this network is made use of for processing transactions made on it.

Can unlimited Bitcoins be created?

According to the Bitcoin protocol, only a finite number of Bitcoins can be created, and once that limit has reached, further Bitcoins cannot be generated.

What is it based on?

Conventional currency is usually backed by some form of precious metal like gold or silver for instance. Theoretically, you are entitled to obtain your money's worth in the precious metal that is used for backing it up. However, nothing of this sort applies to Bitcoins. Bitcoins are backed by mathematical equations and not precious metals. People across the world, known as miners, are making use of dedicated software and computers for solving these mathematical equations for creating blocks of data that results in the creation of Bitcoins. This software is an open source code, and anyone can take a look at these transactions.

Characteristics of a Bitcoin

There are several distinctive features that a Bitcoin has, and they have been discussed in this section.

The Bitcoin is a decentralized medium of exchange, and this implies that it is not under the control of a regulatory authority. Every machine that is capable of mining and processing Bitcoin transactions automatically becomes a part of the Bitcoin global network. All the machines will be working together. Theoretically, this implies that no single authority has the power to take away Bitcoins from others. Even if the network does go offline due to some reason, the money will keep flowing, and nothing will interrupt this flow.

All banks that form a part of the conventional system of banking have a multistage procedure for opening a simple bank account. Setting up a merchant account is even more cumbersome than a regular account. However, when it comes to this cryptocurrency, a user can set up a Bitcoin address within no time and without the payment of any unnecessary fees. This network offers anonymity as well. Users can set up multiple Bitcoin addresses, and none of these addresses are linked to any names, addresses, or other personal information. The functioning of the Bitcoin is very transparent. Every transaction that takes place is recorded within the network in the form of a ledger, and this ledger is open for public viewing.

This ledger forms a part of the blockchain. If your Bitcoin address happens to be public, then anyone can view the number of Bitcoins you are holding onto, but no one will be privy to the information regarding the ownership of that address. There are different measures that a user can take for making sure that their activities are protected online. A transactional fee is chargeable by banks whenever you make a transaction, and this doesn't happen while dealing with Bitcoins. You can transfer money anywhere in the world, and the receiver will also be able to receive it within no time. Once a Bitcoin has been debited from your account, there is no way in which that transaction can be reversed, unless the recipient has sent them back to you. If not, your Bitcoins are gone forever.

It does seem like Bitcoin has got a lot going on for it, doesn't it? How does it all work in practice though? You will learn more about Bitcoins in the coming chapters.

What makes it different?

Bitcoins can be used for buying things electronically. In this sense, they are similar to fiat currencies that can be traded as well. However, the primary distinction between these two is that Bitcoins are decentralized in nature.

How are Bitcoins made?

Bitcoin is made up of data files that are collectively known as the blockchain. Every blockchain consists three parts. The first two help in identifying the address and for recording the history of people trading Bitcoins. This makes up the ledger portion of Bitcoin. The third part of the blockchain technology consists a private key header log. The header is the complex part of this technology, and it helps in confirming a transaction by recording the unique digital signature that was used.

Every signature that's used is different, and it corresponds with the wallet it has been linked to. The security system of this cryptocurrency consists of different digital signatures that can be tracked and traced on the Internet since this forms part of the publicly available information present on the blockchain. These files are anonymous, and they don't reveal the identity of the user and are displayed in the form of a number that the Bitcoin wallet is associated with for conducting a transaction. The blockchain doesn't record the identity of the user, and the Bitcoin will be present in either your wallet or the cloud. Only the accounting information is available on the public ledger. The history of every single Bitcoin transaction that ever took place is public information, and this layer of added transparency deters anyone from making use of Bitcoins for any illegal purposes.

Getting familiar with Bitcoins

People are still in the process of warming up to the idea of cryptocurrencies. The attitude displayed by the general public is similar to that they had towards the Internet during the 90's or online shopping during the early 2000s. Change of any kind doesn't appeal to the general human nature, and it takes a while for the masses to accept any new technology as a part of their daily lives. Bitcoins, when they were introduced, were considered to be a disruptive financial force that's well ahead of its time.

This general attitude can obstruct the further development and advancement of brilliant technology like the Bitcoins. However, there has been an increase in the portion of the public that is welcoming this futuristic currency. Bitcoin allows the user to transfer funds to anyone anywhere in the world without having to worry about the involvement of middlemen. Bitcoin was created with the aim of creating a currency that will help in shifting the power of control to the individual dealing with it and not any other regulatory body. Bitcoin isn't a currency in its strict sense of meaning, but it is a method of digitized payment that can be used for acquiring different goods and services online. Existing businesses have the option of conducting their transactions by using cryptocurrency as well as fiat money.

The process of setting up a Bitcoin wallet is simple and doesn't need any additional infrastructure. There are no additional costs that are involved for accepting payments made in Bitcoins. Once you have Bitcoins in your possession, you can easily convert them into any of the local currencies you want, and the same can be easily transferred to your bank account. Users have the option of purchasing this cryptocurrency directly, or they can use other cryptocurrencies for obtaining the same.

About the Blockchain

The best possible manner in which one can understand the Bitcoin blockchain is by comparing it a transactional ledger that is publicly available. This helps in ensuring transparency in operations by handing the control over the entire system of accounting to the general public. The blockchain helps in recording, compiling, and verifying all the Bitcoin transactions that have and still are taking place since its conceptualization almost a decade ago. Every transaction that was ever made has to be verified and only then will it be recorded on the existing blockchain.

Since it is present in a decentralized form, there isn't a single point from which the whole network can be razed to the ground. The data is processed and recorded not just by one authority, but also by tens of thousands of users spread all over the world. This distribution of power and information make the network infallible to the threat of hacking or theft.

The blockchain comprises of huge blocks of data that helps in recording and verifying every transaction that's ever occurred. The network is always aware of all transactions relating to every single coin ever produced, and every coin is accounted for on it as well. The blockchain is a public ledger that records all the past and present transactions and all the transactions that will take place in the future as well. It is similar to bookkeeping. Bookkeeping is an essential aspect of the functioning of any organization, and this is usually private information. However, when it comes to Bitcoins, this information is public. This doesn't mean that the feature of anonymity is lost. The identity of the user is never divulged. The blockchain just keeps track of all transactions and the transaction when recorded on the blockchain is only recorded in the form of wallet addresses. The identity of the owner is always secure. So, security is ensured while improving transparency.

The blockchain is a public database of all Bitcoin transactions. A Bitcoin node on the network is a computer that is running a wallet application and is used for detecting and validating every new transaction that involves Bitcoins. Every single node on the network will have access to the entire transactional history of Bitcoins. The blockchain network keeps on increasing whenever a new block is added to it after it has been verified and recorded by these nodes. Every new block that's added will consist of a summary of the previous block on the network. Once a block has been added to the network, it cannot be altered. In 2013, it was recorded that the blockchain has more than 50Gb data on it.

How to compete for coins?

A miner will thus seal a block, and all miners compete with each other for doing this. There is a particular software that they tend to make use of for mining blocks of data. Every time a miner has generated a hash, such miner will receive 25 Bitcoins as a reward. The blockchain is constantly updated, and whenever it is updated, every miner on the network will get to know about it. The incentive of receiving Bitcoins keeps the miners interested while securing the entire network. A small snag in this is the ease with which a hash can be produced. Computers are good at this. So, to make it slightly more difficult, the Bitcoin protocol was designed in such a way that it makes this process quite difficult by something that's known as "proof of work."

This protocol doesn't accept any old hash that's created, and there are some criteria that have to be fulfilled. The hash of a block should look in a particular way, and it has to consist a specific number of zeroes in the beginning. There is no possible manner in which it can be determined how a hash has to look until after it has been produced. As and when a new piece of data is added to the mix, the hash will transform too. Miners aren't allowed to interfere with an existing transaction on the block. They should instead change the manner in which the data is being used for creating a hash. They do this by making use of a random piece of data known as a nonce. A nonce is made use of in a transaction for creating its hash. If the hash cannot fit into the given format, then the nonce will have to be changed, and the entire thing needs to be formatted again. It usually takes numerous attempts for finding the perfect nonce that can fit the given requirements and all the miners on the network will keep trying till they find the perfect fit. And once someone obtains the correct hash, all miners will get to know.

The Bitcoin network is an exclusive ecosystem, and it helps in storing value digitally. People have the option of saving their Bitcoins within their digital wallets and can enter into a transaction without relying on any third parties or regulatory authority. Once you have your Bitcoins with you and you have secured them, then it is virtually impossible for anyone to take these away from you. The government or any other regulatory authority has no power to take them away from you, they cannot freeze your Bitcoin account, and they certainly cannot stop you from transacting over the Bitcoin network. Whenever you are giving your credit or debit card to a vendor or even a merchant, then you are automatically giving them access to your credit line, regardless of the amount involved in the transaction. All these modes of payment operate on a pull basis and once the payment has been initiated the funds are automatically pulled from your account. Cryptocurrencies function on a push basis, and this means that only the holder of these cryptocurrencies is equipped with sending the exact amount to the merchant and no one else can do this.

Buying Bitcoins

Now that you have learned the basics of Bitcoins, the next step would be to buy some Bitcoins. How do you buy Bitcoins? In this chapter, you will learn more about buying Bitcoins. You can purchase Bitcoins from Bitcoin exchanges or buy them directly from others. There are different ways in which you can pay for them as well, and they range from cash to credit card payments, wire transfers, or making the purchase with other cryptocurrencies, depending on where and whom you are buying it from. It might not be easy to buy Bitcoins with a credit card or your PayPal account depending on where you reside. The reason for this is quite simple. A transaction like this can be reversed with simple phone call to the credit card company.

It is quite difficult to prove that any goods had ever exchanged hands when Bitcoins are transferred. This is the main reason why exchanges tend to avoid this form of payment, and even most of the private sellers would agree. However, the number of options that most of the consumers has increased these days. In the United States, Coinbase and Circle are two services that allow for the purchase of Bitcoins with credit cards. In the UK, Bittylicious, CoinCorner, and Coinbase are accepting credit and debit cards of the Visa and MasterCard networks. All the underbanked consumers residing in the US can opt for Expresscoin. It accepts money orders, wire transfers as well as personal checks.

Wallets

The first thing that you will need to do would be to get yourself a wallet for your Bitcoins. After this, you will require a place for storing your Bitcoins. In the world of cryptocurrencies, a wallet is made use of for storing your Bitcoins. These wallets are quite similar to a bank account that you might have. Depending on the level of security that you are looking for, different wallets are available. Some are like regular spending accounts that are similar to a regular wallet that you carry with you and then there are others that have got a high level of security.

Bitcoin exchanges

There are plenty of Bitcoin exchanges as well as wallets to choose from. There are proper exchanges for institutional traders, and then there are wallet services that are available for someone who is just testing the waters. Most of the exchanges, as well as wallets, will store the digital or fiat currency you hold, just like a traditional bank account would. Exchanges and wallets are a really good option if you ever want to engage in trading.

One-on-one meeting

You buy Bitcoins from a local seller. Different websites will allow for such transactions like LocalBitcoins. These sites will allow you to meet up with different traders of Bitcoins, and you can decide whether you want to finalize the trade or not.

Mining Bitcoins

The next method in which you can own Bitcoins would be by mining them. You need a PC and a powerful graphics card to get started with mining your Bitcoins. There are certain mining specific devices that are referred to as ASICs. The number of Bitcoins still available is steadily dwindling down as time progresses. This means that mining isn't as cost-effective as it was a year ago. Most people end up spending more on the hardware and electricity than what they could ever earn from mining. Mining is usually done in pools these days. This means a couple of miners would get together and pool their resources for mining Bitcoins and then divide the rewards according to a predetermined ratio.

Bitcoin ATMs

This is a new concept, and it is slowly picking up speed. This is quite similar to a face-to-face exchange, but it involves a machine. You will have to insert your currency or scan the QR code of your wallet, and you will receive the necessary codes for loading Bitcoins into your Bitcoin wallet. Exchange rates can vary, and it can be anywhere between 3-8%. Buying Bitcoins might not seem like an easy thing to do, especially for newcomers. However, the number of avenues available for buying these Bitcoins from is increasing.

Chapter 6 - Bitcoin Investing Strategies

There are three simple steps that you should always follow while investing in Bitcoins and these have been explained in this chapter.

Always have a plan

If you are interested in becoming a successful investor, then make sure that you always have a strategy in mind. A strategy or a plan would depend on your financial goal. Maybe you want to take up investing for paying off your student debt, for creating a retirement plan, or maybe for some other reason. Having a goal in mind will help you in coming up with a plan with sufficient risk-reward tradeoff. For instance, a student looking to pay off the student loans can invest $100 for now with the potential of repaying the loans off within 4 years. If you are interested in securing your future post-retirement and have a steady job, for now, the amount that you are willing to invest will increase as well.

Also, the risk you are willing to take on will differ depending on your goals.

Price drops are common

Bitcoin is a volatile cryptocurrency, and it can experience several price changes. This is quite common with any investment. The price of a Bitcoin can drop faster than anything else due to its volatile nature. You need to be prepared for any fluctuations in its price. Its value will not be constant and don't get scared when it feels like the price has decreased slightly. This happens because no one knows if this new technology will overthrow the existing financial system or just give it a new makeover.

Always secure you Bitcoins

The owner of a Bitcoin has complete control over their funds. Where there is power, responsibility is bound to follow suit. You need to understand that you are probably your worst enemy. It isn't just the threat of hacking and theft that you should be wary of. Selling your Bitcoins at a low price is certainly a bad idea, and panic selling is even worse. Poor investment decisions and lapse of security can incur you a major loss. Your

Bitcoins should always be stored in a secure wallet and take utmost care while doing so. Follow all the safety and security protocols. Don't give your private key to anyone. Also, don't forget your security. If you do, then you cannot retrieve your Bitcoins.

Chapter 7 - All About Ethereum

The first cryptocurrency created was Bitcoin. Only after Bitcoin became a success, did the idea of inventing other cryptocurrencies come up. Bitcoin is a type of digital currency, and it doesn't have a tangible form. Bitcoins can be made use of for buying things electronically. Cryptocurrencies are similar to the traditional fiat currency, save that they exist in a digital form and are decentralized. Ethereum aims to function as a decentralized Internet and also as a decentralized app store, that will provide support for Dapps along the way. Ethereum isn't "owned" by anyone, but the network that supports it isn't free. The network makes use of "ether."

Ether is a code that is used to pay for the computational resources necessary to run an application or a program. Ether is quite similar to Bitcoin, and it is a bearer asset. Ether doesn't need a third party to process or approve a transaction. It doesn't operate the way digital currency or the payment system works, and it instead focuses on providing "fuel" that will help in the functioning of Dapps on this network. It might seem slightly complicated; however, it isn't. Dapps is like an online notebook for deleting, posting, or modifying a note and you will have to pay a transaction fee in the form of Ether to make the necessary changes. Therefore, Ether has also been referred to as digital oil.

Let us take this analogy a little ahead, then the transaction fees is calculated by the amount of gas required for the action. The transactional cost will depend on the computational power necessary and the time required to get it up and to run. A transaction that will cost 500 gas will be paid in Ether. Thinking of Ethereum from an economic perspective is quite open-ended. There is a cap that is set on Bitcoins, whereas no such limit applies to Ether.

In 2014, about 60 million Ether was purchased by the users who participated in the crowdfunding campaign. About 12 million Ether went towards the Ethereum Foundation that comprises of researchers and developers responsible for keeping the ether network going on. 5 Ethers are allocated to a miner every 12 seconds for verifying a transaction that took place on the network. A maximum of 18 million Ethers can be mined in each year, and a new block is created o the network every 12 seconds.

The popularity of cryptocurrencies surged once again after the rate per Ether had risen to over $400. That's a 5000% increase in its value. The wealth that is produced by this ever-expanding industry is difficult to comprehend, especially when it is difficult to see where the value of this currency is originating. In this section, let us take a look at a deeper look into what Ethereum is all about and how it fares in comparison to Bitcoin.

Ethereum did not appear out of thin air, regardless of what its name might suggest. It makes use of the similar blockchain technology that Bitcoin uses. However, its platform is Turing-complete, and this is the reason why it is also referred to as programmable blockchain. This implies the scope for developing better functionality and advanced applications, including other cryptocurrencies as well. While on the other hand, Bitcoin just has one function. It is a type of digital currency that helps in peer-to-peer transactions. The first cryptocurrency that made use of the blockchain technology was Bitcoin. The limited function and scope offered by Bitcoin have created scaling issues for itself.

The important features of the Ethereum blockchain network are smart contracts and Ethereum Virtual Machine. These features are the reason why Ethereum network is so much more than just a regular system of payment that makes use of digital currency. Contracts that are written in code and are considered to be self-executing are known as Smart Contracts.

Other blockchain technologies are capable of executing a Smart Contract, Ethereum has this feature embedded into his payment system, it allows for immediate transfer of value across the global market this is decentralized with zero-downtime, and there are no middlemen involved in this process.

The Bitcoin was created with the intention of being used for the transfer of monetary value. According to the creators of Ethereum, it merely acts as the "gas or fuel" for Smart Contracts. Ethereum can be made use of as a tool of accumulation and transmission of value (it does this with faster transactions than the ones that are offered by the blockchain network of Bitcoins). However, initially, the ETH was intended not just for this but also for providing some functionality to the Smart Contracts (the contract initiators will need to spend some amount in the form of Ether for this purpose, and it can be compared to the transaction fees or the commission charge that banks levy while facilitating a contract

The Ethereum Virtual Machine also referred to, as EVM is a universal computer. The EVM provides its developers the ability not just to operate but even execute almost any kind of application over this network and decentralizes the network.

If there is an attack, the decentralization and the distribution of information in the form of identical blocks that are secured cryptographically across the whole network help Ethereum in getting rid of all the vulnerable points that most of the servers forming the backbone of the Internet suffer from.

Are you also wondering why GPUs can be made use of for mining Ether efficiently but not Bitcoin? Well, the answer lies in the consensus algorithm that has been designed for Ethereum. The network that Ethereum makes use of has an algorithm that is referred to as Ethash. Ethash is ASIC resistant, and it is PoW (proof of work) algorithm. To merely state things the miners will be entitled to receiving blockchain rewards or Ether because of Ethash by computing a few transactions that have been selected randomly.

According to the whitepaper on Ethereum, this design has two outcomes. The first one is that the Ethereum contracts can use any form of computation, so the ASIC of Ethereum would be an ASIC for general computation that is it will be a better CPU. The second outcome is that the process of mining would require the miner to access the entire blockchain and this means that they will need to store the entire blockchain to verify the transactions that take place. This means that it is not necessary for centralized mining pools.

Founded by Vitalik Buterin

In the year 2013 Vitalik Buterin had come up with the idea of creating Ethereum while being an active participant in the Bitcoin community. The first white paper he published on Ethereum helped in paving the way for creating Ethereum. Along with Dr. Gavin Wood in the year 2014, he co-founded Ethereum. The formal announcement about Ethereum was made by Buterin in Miami at the North American Bitcoin Conference in January of 2014. The yellow paper created by Dr. Gavin in April in the same year serves as a technical guide for the same. After this, Ethereum has been integrated into various programming languages like Java and JavaScript that have improved the performance of the software.

It is available on different platforms

Ether is actively traded on different platforms, and it is not restricted to just one platform. Here are a few platforms that offer different ways for trading ETH. If you are skeptical about risking all your hard-earned money, but you still want a share of the action-taking place, then there is a platform that would fit the bill. Trading Game helps you in trading in Ethereum without any additional costs, and it is a free application. So, all that you will need to do would be get started with exploring the features of this application. Poloniex is a trading platform that has recorded the highest trading volume. Poloniex holds a considerable portion of the Ether market, and it offers several currency pairs like ETH/USDT, ETH/BTC, ETC/BTC, and so on. This platform also allows for trading of Ethereum Classic.

Origin of the name "Ethereum."

The founder of Ethereum, Buterin had come across the term Ethereum when he was glancing through a list of elements listed in science fiction. Vitalik liked the word ether and the meaning associated with it. Ether means air, and it also represents a medium that is permeable to light. If you were interested in playing WoW, then you would have perhaps wondered if he got the idea of the name "Ethereum" from the ethereal race in the game that resides in Netherstorm. Any link from this game to Ethereum is purely incidental and nothing more than it.

The steady increase in price

The original price of Ether was 200 ETH for everyone BTC, which meant one ETH was worth a couple of cents at the most. Things sure did change for Ethereum. The trading price of Ethereum in July 2017 was recorded at $407. This means that there has been an almost 5000% rise in the price of ETH. The second largest cryptocurrency in the world is Ethereum, and it is right behind Bitcoin that has been valued at $48.9 billion. The current market value of Ethereum is pretty high, and it has got huge growth potential. Ethereum and Bitcoin are rivals like you must be aware, and it will be quite interesting to see Ethereum functioning at its full capacity. Analysts are quite sure that the price of Ethereum is bound to increase rather steeply by the end of 2017. One thing that all analysts would agree on would be that Ethereum has got a bright future ahead of itself.

Relation between Ethereum and banks

Taking into consideration the nature of banking industry and also the high level of security that banks will need for protecting their interest as well as their customer's interest, it can be said that Ethereum can be helpful for banks. The value of Ethereum will keep on increasing as banks start moving towards applications based on blockchain technology that uses Smart Contracts for automating the financial process. As the demand for Smart Contracts will increase, the value of Ethereum will increase as well. At present, there are about 11 major banks like Barclays, UBS, HSBC, and many more. These banks have got together with R3 (a startup and an innovation firm that aims at uplifting the role of technology in routine operations) for testing a system. This system will help banks in making use of blockchain for the sake of trading. This test is crucial because it makes use of the blockchain technology that is developed by Ethereum for enabling a Microsoft platform to run on it. If this test turns out to be a success, then not only will it mean that Ethereum will be incorporated into the banking system of these banks, but also revolutionize the entire banking system.

Platform

Frontier was the initial version of Ethereum, and it was a beta release that provided the developers with a platform for experimenting and learning before they can get started with the creation of decentralized apps and tools that were based on Ethereum. On 30th July in the year 2015, Frontier was launched. The next version of Ethereum that was released was known as a homestead, and it was published on 14th March in the year 2016 (on the Pi Day). This was the first ever production release of Ethereum. This upgrade had plenty of changes made to the protocol and the networking change that allowed for further updates in the network. Two more steps are on their way, and their release date hasn't been confirmed yet. The third phase is known as Metropolis and the fourth one as Serenity.

Ether or ETH holds the second largest part of the cryptocurrency market, right after Bitcoin. During the first quarter of 2017, the market share of Ether has increased by $7 billion, and its price has increased more than five times. When compared to its performance in 2015, the value of ETH has grown more than 2800% since that year. The volume of trade taking place in Ether has been fluctuating, and it will keep on doing so. Ether has got great potential, and this is reflected in its present worth. Ether wasn't an overnight success, it has indeed come a long way since it started and it is bound to go further.

Buying Ethereum

Creating an account on the exchange
Like with any other cryptocurrencies, even Ethereum needs to be purchased and sold online via exchanges dealing in this. There are plenty of trading platforms. The most popular options

include Kraken, BitStamp, Coinbase, and Gemini. Before you can start trading in Ethereum, you will need to select an exchange and then create an account on it.

Verifying the account

A good exchange will need for you to verify your account in multiple ways. You might be required to upload a couple of documents for verifying your identity and ensuring that your account clears all the necessary regulations. Verification can take a day or two, and it would depend on how popular and busy the exchange that you have opted for actually is.

Depositing fiat currency

The next step would be to deposit fiat currency into the account through your bank or even a wire transfer. This would take a day or two for the money to get clearance.

Start trading

When your account is verified, and money has also been deposited in it, then you can start purchasing or trading in Ether and other cryptocurrencies as well. The interface of each exchange would be different, and you need to have some patience for getting all the necessary clearances and for confirming the transactions.

Chapter 8 - Litecoin 101

We live in the age of digital currency. Cryptocurrency is no longer an obscure concept. In June 2017, a single Bitcoin was valued at more than $2000. The world of cryptocurrency isn't just restricted to Bitcoins! Did you know that there are about 180 currencies that are in circulation and are recognized internationally? Just like standard currency, different types of cryptocurrencies are in existence. Since Bitcoin happens to be the first cryptocurrency, it enjoys more publicity than the rest.

Litecoin is the new form of digital currency on the block, and it is poised for dynamic growth. In October 2013, Litecoin was unveiled by Charles Lee, a former Google engineer. It was introduced as the "silver" to the "gold" of Bitcoin. Lee got the idea of Litecoin to fix the problems that Bitcoins posed. Litecoin is amongst the top 5 digital currencies and is said to be a fierce rival of Bitcoin. Litecoin, like several of its counterparts, functions as an online payment system like PayPal or any banking application. Users can efficiently conduct transactions using cryptocurrency. Only instead of using fiat currency like the U.S. dollar, the transaction is conducted in units of Litecoin.

Initially, the world of cryptocurrencies might seem intimidating. If you are equipped with the right information, you can make an informed decision. There are plenty of cryptocurrencies to choose from. However, investing in Litecoin is a smart move. In this chapter, you will learn more about what Litecoin is all about, the way it came into existence and some of its basic features.

How is the Litecoin made?

Litecoin, like all the other cryptocurrencies, and therefore it is not issued by a government or any other regulatory authority. Throughout the history, governments and banks were entrusted with the responsibility of minting money. At least that's how things have been until the invention of cryptocurrencies. Litecoins aren't regulated by the Federal Reserve and certainly aren't minted at the Bureau of Engraving and Printing. Litecoins, like bitcoins need to be mined. This process involves the processing and verification of all the Litecoin transactions that ever took place. There is a cap on the number of Litecoins that can exist, just like other cryptocurrencies and this is one of the differentiating factors between Litecoins and fiat money. Not more than 84 million Litecoins can be in circulation and at present the time taken for generating a single block on the Litecoin network is 2.5 minutes. The block consists of ledger entries of Litecoin transactions that take place anywhere in the world and the Litecoin derives its value from this network. The block of transactions is verified by using special mining software and is visible to all the miners on the Litecoin network. Once a block is successfully verified, the next block will enter the chain, and this would contain the record of all the Litecoin transactions ever transacted.

Mining for Litecoin

The incentive offered for mining is that for every block that is successfully verified, 25 Litecoins are awarded.

Initially, the number of Litecoins provided as a reward was 50, and from October 2015, it's been reduced to 25. This process of reduction will keep on recurring until all the 84 million Litecoins are mined. Will an unscrupulous miner change the algorithm of the block and enable double spending? Well, this isn't possible and any attempt made to do so can be spotted immediately by the other miners.

The identity of any miner that spots such an irregularity is always anonymous. The only way the entire blockchain network can be disrupted it would be if a majority of miners agree to process the false transactions, this is practically impossible to achieve. Mining cryptocurrency at a rate that can be considered to be profitable to the miner would need a lot of processing power and specialized hardware. Your regular laptop isn't designed to be fast enough to complete this task. This is where Litecoins differ from their competitors. Any off-the-shelf computers can mine Litecoins, however, a machine with a higher processing power can help in increasing the chances of earning some Litecoins.

Value of Litecoin

Any currency and even the gold bullion are only as valuable as the society perceives it is. If the Federal Reserve increases the circulation of all the dollars in the market, then the value of the dollar is bound to plummet. This phenomenon isn't just restricted to currency. When the supply of any good or service increases, then there will be a reduction in its value. The creators of Litecoin were aware of this. They knew it would be difficult for a new currency to build a good reputation for itself. However, by restricting the number of Litecoins in supply, the founders managed to put people's fear about overproduction to rest.

In a way, Litecoins are derived from Bitcoins. You can obtain Litecoins by creating an account for trading your Bitcoins for Litecoins at an online exchange for cryptocurrencies. You must be wondering why you should trade one cryptocurrency for another? There are certain advantages that Litecoin has got over Bitcoins. Litecoin is capable of handling a greater number of transactions because the time required for the generation of a block is less. The transaction fee is less as well. So, the value of Litecoin is dependent on the perception of the society. The most reliable store of value during a crisis would be the currencies used. During the late 1990s and early 2000s, Zimbabwean was hit hard by hyperinflation, and the Zimbabwean dollar had become worthless. Everyone who was holding any form of liquid assets suffered a significant loss. This scenario is almost impossible to think about when using Litecoins because of the cap on the number of Litecoins in circulation.

Why is Litecoin unique?
Bitcoin has got a leg up on its competition since it was the first digital currency created. However, its early arrival has also resulted in a couple of drawbacks. Developers of all the significant cryptocurrencies have managed to identify the weaknesses present in Bitcoins and tweak their currencies for overcoming these

shortcomings. Bitcoin was the first one to use Blockchain technology. However, Litecoin has managed to overcome specific issues that plagued its predecessor.

The foundation of all cryptocurrencies in existence is the Blockchain technology. Every transaction that takes place in the network of digital currencies is recorded within a block. All these blocks are linked together to form a literal chain. Anyone on the network has got access to the information that is present on this Blockchains. This implies that the transactions are available for public viewing, even if the user is anonymous.

This framework helps in making cryptocurrencies secure. Litecoin uses this technology more efficiently. On the Litecoin network, a new block is generated every 2.5 minutes, which is 7.5 times faster than the Bitcoin network. All those merchants who are looking for faster transactions will find this appealing. Transactions with Litecoin aren't just swift; they are secure as well. Segregated Witness, popularly known as SegWit was activated in the blockchain network of Litecoin. In this process, obtaining signature data from transactions breaks down the blocks in a blockchain. Litecoin can process lightning-fast payments because of this. In the world of cryptocurrency, only a finite number of coins can exist. There cannot be more than a specific number of Bitcoins that are present in the world. The same rule applies to Litecoins as well. However, the number of coins present can vary, and this works in Litecoin's favor.

The Scrypt algorithms that Litecoin makes use of makes it easier for miners to access the network. This can have two outcomes. The first one is that it would encourage more miners to participate in the Litecoin network. This will help in promoting the usage of Litecoin since it is attractive to all those users who never got an opportunity to mine Bitcoin. The simplicity of the Litecoin mining process is attractive to Bitcoin miners. Bitcoin mining needs specialized supercomputers, and these algorithms are just increasing in complexity. So, all those miners who are tired of struggling with Bitcoin mining can shift to Litecoin now.

Investing in Litecoin

Litecoin is a dominant digital currency, and with the way that it is progressing, it has got a lot of potential. If you are thinking about investing in Litecoin, then now is the time. You can purchase these from any of the exchanges or mine them. More information about both these methods has been provided in the coming chapters.

Like mentioned earlier, Litecoin was developed as an alternative to Bitcoin to address some of its shortcomings. Litecoin is lightweight and is more abundant when compared to Bitcoin. The proof-of-work algorithm used by Litecoin is Scrypt, and this algorithm is almost immune to ASIC mining. You will learn more things about getting started with Litecoins in the coming chapters. Here are a few things that you should take into consideration before buying Litecoin.

This cryptocurrency has become quite popular amongst the speculators in the market after the price surge that the Bitcoin experienced in November 2013. The prices of these cryptocurrencies might move similarly. However, the prices of Litecoin are comparatively lower.

The infrastructure of Litecoin is relatively less developed than that of Bitcoin. This might not be a problem for a seasoned investor, but a novice investor might take a while to figure things out. You can earn Litecoins by mining them by using standard computing equipment.

You should always do plenty of research on your own, before investing your hard-earned money, and never take on more risk than that you can shoulder.

Cash for Litecoins or Bitcoins for Litecoins?

Once you have made up your mind about buying Litecoins, you will need to decide whether you will want to buy these in exchange for fiat currency or Bitcoins. The infrastructure of Litecoin isn't as developed as that of Bitcoin. The easiest manner in which you can acquire

Litecoins would be by buying them with Bitcoins. This is the fastest method, and for most of the users, this is cost effective as well. If you are holding Bitcoins, then you can make use of these for buying Litecoins from any of the listed exchanges like BTC-e, Kraken, Cryptsy, and other transactions.

The process of buying Litecoins is yet to be streamlined. There are about two dozen exchanges that deal in Litecoins and most of them allow for only Bitcoin to Litecoin transactions or vice versa. Couple of exchanges like Bitfinex, Crypto-Trade, Kraken, and BTC-e sell Litecoins for fiat currency (dollars, euros, and rubles only). However, the availability would depend on your location. For instance, in the UK, the investors have the option of directly buying Litecoins from Bittylicious or BitBargain via a banking transfer. However, this isn't the case in most of the countries.

It might seem straightforward to purchase Litecoin by a fiat wire transfer, but this can be quite tedious. Some of the major Bitcoin exchanges aren't yet open to the idea of trading in Litecoin. The obvious advantage of buying Litecoin with Bitcoin should be speed. Theoretically, this should just take a couple of minutes; whereas international wire transfers can take up to a few days and these transfers are usually subjected to several additional costs as well. There aren't many Litecoin exchanges, and this means that all the interested investors will have to rely on international transfers. A viable alternative would be buying Bitcoin locally, thereby skipping the hassle of international money transfer, and converting the same into Litecoin.

Litecoin mining

Litecoin uses a proof-of-work algorithm that is entirely different from the one that Bitcoin makes use of. Litecoin uses Scrypt hashing algorithm. This algorithm was designed in such a manner that it would be difficult to execute a large-scale hardware attack because of the large quantities of memory this would require. Litecoin mining is a complicated process, and it goes beyond simply checking the blocks of Litecoin transactions. Most people end up spending more on the hardware and electricity than what they could ever earn from mining. Mining is usually done in pools these days. This means a couple of miners would get together and pool their resources for mining Litecoins and then divide the rewards according to a predetermined ratio. This certainly isn't for hobbyists.

Litecoin wallets

Block.io:

This provides a multi-signature wallet to all the Litecoin users. This means that for a transaction to be authorized, two or more signatures would be required. One would be the signature of the user, and the other would be the signature of the company. This also implies that the private keys of every wallet would be stored by the team operating at Block.io and this might be a turn-off for a lot of people. However, it offers more convenience since it supports HD wallet. Apart from Litecoin, it can be used for Bitcoin and Dogecoin as well.

Exodus:

This wallet supports different cryptocurrencies like Litecoin, Bitcoin,

Dash, Ether, Dogecoin, and Golem as well. It offers full control to the user over their private keys. It is an open source wallet.

LoafWallet:

If you have a device that can support iOS, then this would be a good option for you. It has all the features that a Litecoin investor would want. A functional mobile wallet will cater to the needs of novice and experienced users, and LoafWallet does this. This is a lightweight client, and you don't have to spend hours syncing it with the Blockchain. It makes use of AES hardware encryption and app sandboxing for preventing anyone from inserting their address into a given transaction. What's more? It can be installed onto your Apple Watch as well. If you are looking for functionality, then this is a pretty good option.

Electrum-LTC:

This is a popular wallet amongst Bitcoin users. Now, they have tweaked the codebase for supporting Litecoin too. It makes use of a see passphrase for protecting a wallet and for restoring a wallet from a backup. It can be downloaded for devices supported by Linux, Windows and OSX from the official online site. This is a lightweight wallet, and therefore you needn't wait for hours to sync it with the blockchain. The main advantage of this wallet is its backup feature. Even if the user does lose their Electrum-LTC wallet, it can be retrieved in the app by using the passphrase. There is an option of generating offline wallet for cold storage. Users can also export the address of their private key to another Litecoin wallet.

When you are selecting a wallet for securing your cryptocurrency, make sure that you are prudent.

Buying Litecoin

In this chapter, you will learn about the different ways in which you can buy Litecoins by making use of various payment options. Before you get started with buying Litecoins, you should make sure that you have got a good wallet in which you can store your Litecoins.

Buying with credit or debit card

Coinbase:

This is perhaps the easiest manner in which you will be able to buy Litecoins with your credit card. The purchase fee that is charged is up to 3.99% of a given purchase. This platform is available in US, UK, Europe, Singapore, and Australia. This same platform can also be made use of for buying Litecoins with a bank account or a bank transfer. This option is available in all the above-mentioned countries and Canada as well. Americans can make use of ACH transfer (it'll take about 5 to 7 days), and Europeans can make use of SEPA transfer and the waiting period can range from a day to three days. The fees per transaction are about 1.49%.

Bitpanda:

This is based in Austria, and it is a crypto-brokerage service. Residents of most of the European countries can buy Litecoins by accessing this platform. SEPA can be made use of for transfer from any of the European countries. NETELLER, GiroPay, or SOFORT can be made use of as well for a bank transfer.

Buying Litecoin with cash

There is no good way in which you can buy Litecoins with cash. The most popular manner for acquiring Bitcoins instead of cash would be via LocalBitcoins. However, this platform doesn't support Litecoin as of now. The other Bitcoin exchanges that are quite popular are BitQuick and Wall of Coins, and neither of these are Litecoin compatible. This means that you will need first to purchase Bitcoins with cash and then exchange these for Litecoin by making use of the methods mentioned above. The same would apply to Bitcoin ATMs as well. Most of them don't support Litecoin. So, if you are interested in buying Litecoin at a Bitcoin ATM, you will need to purchase Bitcoin and then convert them into Litecoin.

Buying Litecoin with PayPal

Just like buying Litecoin with cash, there is no direct way in which you can buy Litecoin with PayPal. You will have to acquire Bitcoin by making use of PayPal, and once you have acquired

Bitcoins, you will need to convert them into Litecoin. The process of acquiring Bitcoin with PayPal is quite extensive.

Buying Litecoin with Bitcoin

If you are already in possession of Bitcoins, then it is very easy to convert these into Litecoins. You will need to find an exchange that deals in LTC/BTC transactions. Most of the exchanges deal in such transactions because they are quite popular.

Changelly: This is perhaps the fastest method that is available for the conversion of Bitcoin to Litecoin. You will just have to enter the number of Litecoin you will want to buy and provide the Litecoin address. Then this platform does the calculations and will inform you the number of Bitcoins that will be necessary for the exchange and the address to which the Bitcoins should be sent. Once you do this, the LTC will be automatically sent to your wallet after a little while.

Buying Litecoin with Skrill

BiPanda also accepts Skrill payments for acquiring Litecoins. The fee will vary and will be included in your buying price.

Buying Litecoin with Ethereum

2017 has been quite a lucky year for Ethereum, and this cryptocurrency has witnessed a massive surge in its prices. Ethereum holders can trade in their ether for buying Litecoin. Litecoin has got a very good rate of liquidity, and it is quite popular among traders, especially in China. In this section, let us take a look at some of the popular exchanges that you can make use of for converting your Ethereum into Litecoin.

Changelly:

This is perhaps the most unique exchange there is, and it is also a fast way in which you can convert Ethereum into Litecoin. When you are making use of Changelly, you needn't have to store your money with the exchange (third-party), and this reduces your exposure to the risk of theft. You will merely have to specify the number of Litecoin you will want to buy, specify the address to which the Litecoin needs to be sent. Changelly will do the calculations and will inform you of the number of

Ethereum that would be required for this purchase. They will provide an address to which Ether will need to be sent, and within a while, you will receive a deposit of Litecoin to your wallet. Any other form of altcoin can also be converted to Litecoin by making use of Changelly, and the same procedure is applicable.

Poloniex:
This is the largest exchange of altcoin in the world. There is one major drawback of making use of Poloniex for converting your Ethereum to Litecoin. Poloniex does not directly assist in the conversion of Ethereum to Litecoin. You will first have to convert your Ethereum to Bitcoin and then convert this Bitcoin to Litecoin. ShapeShift is quite similar to Changelly. In fact, this was the first company that had come up with the concept of exchange for holding onto your funds.

The most frequently asked question about the conversion of Ethereum to Litecoin is "why are there only a few options available?" The basic issue present in all of the crypto markets across the globe is liquidity. As the space increases, the liquidity will also improve. However, as of now, Bitcoin is the only cryptocurrency that enjoys a high rate of liquidity. The other cryptocurrencies will soon follow suit. This is the main reason why most of the options regarding the purchase of Litecoin require Bitcoin and then its conversion or exchange.

Buying Litecoin online

Most of the options that have been mentioned above will allow you to buy Litecoins online. You will have to buy them online if you want to acquire them by making use of your credit card, debit card, bank transfer, or even Skrill. The only option where an online transfer isn't possible is when you are trying to buy them with cash.

Chapter 9 - Cryptocurrency Wallets

A cryptocurrency wallet is a place for the safekeeping of your cryptocurrency. The one feature that distinguishes a cryptocurrency wallet from a regular wallet is that the former is akin to a bank account. There are two types of wallets to choose from- a web-based wallet and a software wallet. The software wallet is quite straightforward. You merely have to install the necessary software and start making use of it. This kind of wallet will provide you with complete control over your cryptocurrency's security. The web wallet, on the other hand, is very simple to use. However, if you are making use of this type of wallet, you will need to place your trust in a third party for the safekeeping of your cryptocurrency. Here are the different options available to you.

Desktop wallets
This wallet will essentially be installed on your PC or your laptop. You can download a cryptocurrency client. There

are different cryptocurrency customers who have managed to write in different programming languages and different tradeoffs. The entire process can take up a couple of days. The wallet has to be synced with all the transactions that are taking place on the blockchain or any other technology that the cryptocurrency makes use of.

Mobile wallets

Mobile clients are often known as light customers and they will need secondary data that can be downloaded from a server for connecting to the network before you can start transacting. Such clients can then download an application onto their smartphones. This option is very convenient, but it isn't the safest one available. This method is quite helpful when you have to store large holdings of cryptocurrencies.

Hardware wallets

Storing your private keys on a device that's not connected to the Internet is known as cold storage. These are quite small, and they don't take up much storage space. These wallets combine the best of the previously mentioned wallets.

Hardware wallets are secure, and they can be detached from the Internet as well. This means that you can authorize transactions without being online. However, if convenience and ease of access are your top priorities, then this might not be the best option that's available.

Paper wallets

Another cold storage wallet option that's available to users is an old-school one. You will simply have to write down or print your private key on a piece of paper and then place this paper in a deposit box or your safe. Online tools can be made use of for providing key pairs to your system, and this tends to make your keys vulnerable if the site is hacked. If you have a cryptographic package installed, then you can make use of it for generating keys by using command line in your preferred language. If you lose your keys, there is no possible manner in which they can be recovered. So, be very careful while using your private keys. If your keys are gone, then you can very well forget about the Bitcoins you are holding. Always create multiple copies of passwords as well as keys and store them in a safe.

There are a couple of risks that are associated with the removal of third parties while transacting. The most important thing that you need to be aware of is that losing your private key is definitely not similar to forgetting your password. You lose your key; you might as well forget about all the cryptocurrency that's stored in your wallet. Forever! The removal of trusted parties while conducting transactions is a double-edged sword. On one hand, it helps in simplifying the process without the unnecessary involvement of middlemen and other intermediaries. However, on the flipside, this means that you won't have anyone to turn to whenever you run into trouble or if you lose your private key. Bearing this in mind, there are different wallets to choose from for storing your cryptocurrency. Make use of two wallets while transacting: one for just holding funds for a short duration and the other for holding your savings. The wallet you are using for holding your savings should be an offline wallet if you want to improve your security.

Depending upon your preferences or convenience and security you can select any of these options. Usually, convenience and security are at odds with one another. The more convenient something is, the less secure it is and vice versa. Well, let us take a look at the top 5-cryptocurrency wallets

Cubits

This was founded in the year 2014, and it is a trading platform for cryptocurrencies. It supports the exchange of Bitcoins for about 17 different types of currencies, and they work along with OKPay, SEPA, Swift, Sofort, and Onlinebanktransfer.com for offering their customers a wide variety of options for buying and selling their Bitcoins. The most important feature of this platform is that it is a full-fledged multi-signature cold storage. This wallet makes use of their cryptocurrencies for transactions thereby making sure that your cryptocurrency is secure in your offline wallet. The cold storage feature offered by them is efficiently encrypted and helps in providing your cryptocurrencies with all the necessary security.

Circle

This certainly is an exciting option, as it works as a fusion. It will convert all the transfers of regular currency like dollars to Bitcoins once transferred in your account, without having to force the sender to buy Bitcoins. It almost functions as a de facto payment platform in addition to a storage wallet. For mitigating the volatility of different cryptocurrencies while transactions were being transacted, Circle absorbed this risk by fixing the interest rates the minute a transaction was started. All the funds of the users held in this are insured.

Coinbase

This is an excellent wallet, and it serves about 2.8 million countries and has spread its operations in over 32 countries with a turnover in Bitcoin exchange amounting to $2.5 billion. This wallet will directly link your bank account to the cryptocurrency exchange for converting cryptocurrency into fiat currency and vice versa. It has a mobile application that's developed for Android and iOS platforms as well as a web browser. All the cryptocurrency that is held within their servers are insured and even they offer a multi-signature vault for ensuring the security of the cryptocurrency that lies within it.

Xapo
This is a simple wallet to use, and it allows the user access to the storage vault within which cryptocurrency is stored. This is based in Hong Kong, and this company offers cold storage for your funds that are encrypted and are locked behind walls made of concrete, steel doors and cages that can block radio waves. What's more? They offer their debit card!

Coinkite
This is an innovative platform that allows its users to transfer Bitcoins via SMS, thereby making transactions much simpler and easier. Coinkite is a multi-signature wallet. It means for each transaction that needs to be approved, a blend of many keys is necessary for authentication. To put it simply, if at all

someone wants to hack your wallet, they will need a set of correct codes that need to be entered at the same time. Thereby making it difficult to steal funds from your wallet.

All the cryptocurrency wallets have different features to offer. Just like you would with a regular wallet, you can select one that would meet your tastes and requirements without compromising on security. Spend some time in short-listing the types of wallets that you can make use of, depending on the different features they offer.

Chapter 10 - How to Invest in Cryptocurrencies

One of the most interesting and rewarding ways in which you can grow your capital is by investing in cryptocurrencies. Media has been hailing Bitcoin as the new gold, the growth potential of cryptocurrencies is unparalleled, and they can hold capital in a better manner than the conventional investment instruments. Here are the three simple questions that you should be able to answer before you can start investing in cryptocurrency.

Which cryptocurrency to choose?
Before you decide to invest in Bitcoin, Litecoin or even Ethereum, you should take some time out to figure out the mind of cryptocurrency would suit your needs. You should be sure of the cryptocurrency that you want to invest in. You will need to do plenty of research on your own and figure out if a currency has the potential of it being used by the public at large. The best thing about a

cryptocurrency is it has a growing community of users. This will help in making sure that there are plenty of investors for a particular cryptocurrency at all points of time. Thus, you can make sure that the value of your holdings will not fall below zero. Since the invention of the Internet, doing research has become quite easy. There are plenty of cryptocurrencies to choose from, so select on that will suit your needs. Depending on what you aim to accomplish, the cryptocurrency that you choose would differ.

Which exchange do I use?

The second question you should be able to answer is about the exchange that you want to make use of. Information about different exchanges along with a list of the most popular exchanges has been provided in this book. A smart thing to do would be to purchase your cryptocurrency from an exchange that a lot of people seem to be making use of. This makes sure that you aren't being scammed. However, be wary, a lot of people offering to sell their cryptocurrencies for peanuts are nothing more than a scam. To steer clear of such issues, make use of a trusted platform.

Select an exchange that has a good reputation and has several other features that can help you in investing. There are some exchanges that provide good customer support service, other provide investing tools and guidance, and then there are some that provide both. While selecting an exchange, you should also take the costs involved in it into consideration. You need to get your value for money. If the deposit and withdrawal costs along with the transactional costs are high, then it clearly defeats the purpose of even registering with an exchange. You will need to create an account with most of the exchanges if you are interested in trading. So, you should take into consideration the time it would be necessary for creating your account. The exchange that you are selecting will also depend on the type of cryptocurrency that you want to invest in. Invest in a trusted exchange with low fees so that you will be able to get value for your money while investing in cryptocurrencies. The platform needs to be secure as well. Since there are plenty of hoax and fake websites on the Internet, opt for an exchange that has been in business for a while and is related to cryptocurrencies for a while now.

Which wallet do I use?

You will need to have a cryptocurrency wallet for not just storing your valuable investment but for transacting as well. Make use of the information that has been provided in the previous chapter for selecting a wallet that you can easily make use of. There are different wallets to choose from and depending on your needs; you can always select one that meets your requirements easily. There are software and hardware wallets. Using a combination of these two is a good idea. Since you are the only one that's responsible for the safekeeping of your cryptocurrency, you should take all the necessary precautions for making sure that all your cryptocurrency is very secure. Depending on your needs you can select a wallet that fulfills your requirements.

Steps for investing

Buying your first crypto

There is no time like the present when it comes to starting something new. The first step while investing is to create an account for yourself with a site like Coinbase, Kraken, or anything else that you are comfortable with for converting your funds into cryptocurrencies. You can link up your credit or debit cards, or even your bank account with any such platform for facilitating the transfer of funds. There are pros and cons of every platform that exists so you should always do plenty of research before trusting a platform. Now that you have made up your mind about the type of cryptocurrency you feel like investing in, then select a platform that is best suited for it.

Finalizing a crypto

The number of options that are available in the market these days is quite overwhelming. Even more so when you are just getting started. At least for the first few investments, make it a point to invest in cryptocurrencies that are quite popular. Like Bitcoin, Ethereum,

Litecoin, dash or ripple. It all depends on the kind of cryptocurrency you want to invest in. Bitcoin is considered to be the gold standard in the world of cryptocurrencies. Most of the cryptocurrencies make use of similar technology for their functioning. Don't opt for any obscure cryptocurrencies, especially when you are making your first purchase. Don't dive headfirst into the world of cryptocurrency investing. Instead, take small steps and get a feel of what you are investing in. Understand the market and the instruments involved. Don't invest all your money in one go.

Storing your crypto
Once you have figured out the crypto that you want to invest in, the next step is to find an ideal wallet for storing the same. Refer to the previous chapter for more information on crypto wallets. Select a wallet that will meet all your requirements.

Keep researching
You can never have too much knowledge about something. Keep researching and learning about all the new developments

that keep taking place in the world of cryptocurrencies. If you have decided to invest in a particular cryptocurrency, then make it a point to make sure that you know all the recent changes taking place in it. Refer to different websites and magazines. Read the newspaper to track any recent changes in that particular cryptocurrency and the way in which it would influence your investment.

There are plenty of social media platforms and blogs that you can refer to. Not just that, you can join different communities dedicated to various cryptocurrencies for making sure that you are learning about crypto and allied topics.

Basic investing principles
Everywhere you look, you have got ideas, opinions, and analysis available about investing. It is everywhere, on the television, Internet, magazines, newspapers and so on. You cannot get away from it. A successful investor might incorporate other's analysis into their analysis before making a decision.

However, the final decision is always based on their research.

There are plenty of cryptocurrencies out there for you to invest in. Lots of them would have the potential for a good investment. However, this doesn't mean that you should invest in them. Invest in a cryptocurrency only when you understand how it functions. If you don't, then you are setting yourself up for failure. No, you don't have to know all the technical aspects of it; you just need to have an idea about how it functions. So, that you know if something is going wrong.

Having a diversified portfolio is essential. It helps in spreading the risk. However, too much diversification is a bad thing. It causes the investor to be spread out too thin. A successful investor would have a diverse portfolio so that their risk is distributed optimally, but will ensure that it isn't so diverse that their resources are spread too thin.

Media plays an active role in promoting investments these days. Invest in a crypto that is well established and has a good team of developers. Learn more about them as well.

If you don't have well-defined goals, then you cannot achieve anything in your life. How will you reach your goals without a well thought out strategy? Luck doesn't play a part when it comes to investing, and it certainly doesn't happen overnight. You will need a good investment strategy. To do that, you will need to determine a few things. Take into consideration your aptitude for bearing risk, the funds you will need, the kind of stocks you want to invest in, the portion of your income you would like to invest, and your exit strategy in case the market crashes.

Chapter 11 - Tips and Tricks for Investing

In this chapter, let us take a look at different tips and tricks that you can make use of while investing in cryptocurrencies.

Keeping separate wallets

If you are using a particular wallet for spending your cryptocurrency as well as your entire holding of cryptocurrency, then you are making yourself a soft target for hackers and thieves. There is no limit on the number of Bitcoin addresses for a Bitcoin wallet held by an individual. Therefore, make it a point to use different Bitcoin addresses for spending your money, your savings, and for receiving Bitcoins as well.

Your web wallet shouldn't hold your savings as well

Web wallets are a secure option, but this doesn't mean that they can't be hacked. If your web wallet can be hacked and you have all your savings in it, then you might as well forget about your Bitcoins.

Web wallets are pretty convenient for usage but make sure that you are using them the way you would use your current or checking account at a bank. It is a safe place for holding small savings that you plan on using in the foreseeable future. Therefore, if you just maintain a small balance and even if the wallet gets hacked, the damage you suffer won't be significant. Cryptocurrencies don't work like a regular credit card. If your card gets stolen, you can report the loss and block it. Whereas if your Bitcoins are stolen, there is no possible manner in which you can regain their possession. You cannot claim anyone, and you cannot contact the police since there is no regulatory authority that you can notify. So, it is impossible to trace lost or stolen cryptocurrencies.

Protect your privacy

You are wholly and solely responsible for your security. Do not at any cost- share your private key with anyone else. Your wallet address is similar to your bank account and taking this analogy further; your private key is like the PIN of your account. Your private key is the authorization required for officiating a transaction. Anyone in possession of this key and your wallet address can siphon the funds from your account. Keeping all these threats aside, wouldn't it be foolish to divulge your personal financial information to a stranger? Well, this is something you shouldn't do. Make use of a mixing service that will facilitate the transfer of funds between both your wallets.

Cold storage

Even if your cryptocurrency is stored in a wallet on your computer, you are still vulnerable. Applications of different wallets tend to store the user data in a particular location that can be predicted easily and this would make your makes your financial information susceptible to any attack that can potentially steal this valuable information. A simple solution to this problem would be to make sure that your private key to your cryptocurrency wallet is always stored on an offline media. This additional security can go a long way in making sure your funds are safe and aren't all lost. You can print it on a piece of paper or even store it as a file on a USB. If you want to transfer your cryptocurrency to your offline wallet, you simply have to scan the QR code and save it elsewhere. Once the balance in your wallet is displayed on the application, you can transfer your cryptocurrency to any address that you want to. You can also get your private keys encrypted. This means that the key would be useless without the encryption password. However, don't forget the password!

Back up

The previous tips will help you in protecting your cryptocurrency from external threats, and this tip will help you in protecting your cryptocurrency from yourself. If you are using your PC or your laptop, then you should have a backup option for the wallet used. The public and private keys of your wallet can be saved in a file. That's all that you will need for retrieving your balance. Once the file containing your wallet keys is safe with you, you can store it anywhere you want to like a flash drive, optical disk or on another medium. You can store it in a cloud-based storage system like the Dropbox or iCloud.

Never invest more than you can afford to lose

When it comes to investing, there is a certain degree of risk that accompanies every trade you ever make. When it comes to cryptocurrency, these are not only volatile but are speculative as well. So, your chances of earning a profit or incurring a loss are equally high as well. Poor decisions can lead to huge losses when you are trading in this instrument. The investment you are making should be something that you are entirely comfortable with. Prepare yourself for the worst that you can expect- losing everything that you invested. A successful investor always diversifies their portfolio. Make it a point to invest in a couple of different types of cryptocurrencies. Never invest more than what you can afford to lose. If you don't do this, then your ability to be prudent and rational can be impaired. This results in something that's known as panic selling, and you will end up increasing your losses.

Set goals for every trade you make

Setting goals for yourself is important. This will help in keeping your head clear especially when the market conditions are volatile. Before you decide to trade in a cryptocurrency, make sure that you have set the limits on the price at which you should take your profits and when you need to cut your losses and get out of the trade. Decide this in advance. Having a plan will help you in staying levelheaded and rational during the highs and lows of the market.

Cryptocurrencies are often referred to as virtual currencies, and their share in the total economy is rapidly increasing. As of now, there are more than 800 cryptocurrencies in existence. Investing in cryptocurrencies isn't an exact science. Unlike a company that publicly trades its stocks, there are no financial statements to go through or compare and therefore it is impossible to calculate their book value. Whether a cryptocurrency is undervalued or not is hard to determine since no intrinsic value is known. Investing in cryptocurrencies can seem quite adventurous, even more so when the risk of a capital loss is quite high. However, if you take some time to study and are patient, then you can make use of specific indicators that will help in limiting your risk exposure, avoid certain potential pitfalls, and gauge for yourself if the cryptocurrency is profitable or not. Here are a couple of leads that you should take into consideration before you think of investing in a cryptocurrency.

Technology
If you are thinking about investing in a programmable currency that you will need a basic understanding of the underly8ing technology. Most of the cryptocurrencies make use of the same code as that of a Bitcoin and are just pale copies of the former. Therefore, the investor tends to take little interest in it, unless the Bitcoin fails, as another cryptocurrency can act as its substitute. Take into consideration the validation system that the blockchain makes use of. Does the cryptocurrency make use of proof of work or evidence of stake? Both are being used simultaneously, or

neither is being used? Does it use any other algorithm for checking the transactions on the blockchain? What's the governance that's involved, if any? What method of scalability is considered? Is the cryptocurrency even making use of a blockchain? Cryptocurrencies that don't possess the same characteristics, as the Bitcoin or those that don't use the same language for programming should be studied closely. Don't assume that all the cryptocurrencies are the same.

The number of tokens created
As an investor, you will be buying tokens, so you should check if the cryptocurrency has a finite number of tokens and if the system is deflationary. The quantum of tokens in existence can increase or decrease the price of the cryptocurrency at any point in time. For instance, Bitcoin and Bitcoin cash can only have 21 million tokens at any point in time. So, this is a scarce resource, and with an increase in their demand, their value is bound to increase as well.

The price of a token

Finding a virtual currency that seems to be promising isn't sufficient, you should also know when to buy it. A cryptocurrency can be purchased before its official launch by participating in an ICO or Initial Coin Offering. However, you need to take into consideration the fact that the price of the currency can drop significantly after the brief high of an ICO. If you have missed the ICO, then don't worry. Just wait till the public attention fades away. The price of a cryptocurrency is bound to increase when it is added to an existing trading platform, is taken up by a popular wallet service, or when it has reached the stage of track record. It is wise to buy these tokens before the happening of any of these events when the price isn't too high, and you still have a safety margin working in your favor. There are different trading platforms, websites, and exchanges that will provide you with the necessary charts for judging the performance of a cryptocurrency.

Website matters

Check whether the cryptocurrency you want to invest in has an official website of its own. Is there any information that is available about its creators or the company that's running the operations? Are there any developers and if yes, then their biographies and any white papers describing the nature of the cryptocurrency in question? If you cannot find all this information, then it is better if you stay away from such currency. What if it turns out to be a Ponzi scam? Don't invest blindly.

Any accusations

If the website of a cryptocurrency doesn't look genuine and looks dodgy, then do some research on your own. The simplest manner to do this would be by simply typing the name of the cryptocurrency in a search engine's search box like Google and read more about it. If you come across anything that's hinting at a scam, read about it. Check for yourself if the information is genuine or not and if the accusations hold true. At times there are false charges that are filed as well. Take into consideration the information you obtain from any official websites of magazines and reports and not just random articles on the web. Your source should be a trustworthy one.

Reddit

A popular community website is Reddit. Cryptocurrency communities often tend to create their subreddits for enabling developers, enthusiasts, traders, and other users of cryptocurrencies for sharing their inputs and views. As an investor, you can go through these platforms for checking how a particular cryptocurrency is performing in the market. For instance, if you discover that the community has grown too quickly or is slowly dying, you should most certainly stay away from it. For instance, if you notice that the number of subscribers of a particular cryptocurrency is organic and the graph is rising regularly and gradually, it shows a genuine interest in the currency. On the other hand, if you notice any irregularities like a rapid decline in the number of subscribers after it has reached a high number or a sudden drop in its price and the decline doesn't stop, then in such a case, steer clear of all such investments.

Slack

The communication platform that's mostly used by the developers of cryptocurrencies is Slack. You can register yourself on this platform and obtain all the necessary information about the performance of the cryptocurrencies and any advancement made in the project.

Also, take into consideration the team of developers who are responsible for creating the cryptocurrency. Make it a point to visit different forums and chat rooms dedicated to a particular cryptocurrency for gathering all the information that you need about it. Do plenty of research before you decide to invest your hard-earned money in any of the cryptocurrencies in existence. A little extra effort can go a long way. Be prudent and be wise!

Chapter 12 - Cryptocurrency Exchanges

What does a cryptocurrency exchange mean?

There are certain cryptocurrency websites where you can sell, purchase or trade cryptocurrencies for any other form of digital or traditional currency. These sites are referred to as cryptocurrency exchanges. For those who are interested in trading professionally and want access to trading tools, then they will need a cryptocurrency exchange that requires an ID and an account for operating. If you are interested in trading occasionally or casually, then there are platforms that you can make use of without creating a trading account.

Types of exchanges

There are a couple of types of exchanges that you can make use of like-

Trading platforms
All the websites that connect different buyers and sellers. These websites charge a fee on every transaction that takes place.

Direct trading
These websites are designed to offer a direct person-to-person trading platform where individuals from anywhere in the world can gather to exchange currencies. Direct trading exchanges don't have a market price, and instead, each seller has the option of setting their exchange rate.

Brokers
These are the websites that anyone interested in buying cryptocurrencies can visit, and buy the currency at a listed price. Cryptocurrency brokers are quite similar to the dealers of foreign exchange.

Things to consider

Before you think about trading, there are a couple of things that you need to take into consideration. You should do your homework about the following things before you make your first trade.

Reputation:
The best way to gather information about a particular exchange is to search about it from the reviews given by individual users and also well-known websites providing information about the industry. You can enquire about it on other platforms and forums like Reddit or BitcoinTalk. Refer to financial and economic magazines and blogs for gathering all the necessary information.

Fees:
Most of the exchanges do provide information about the chargeable fees on a transaction, and you should be able to find this on the related website. Before joining a platform, make sure that you understand their policies regarding deposits, transactions, and even withdrawal fees. Depending on the exchange and your usage, the fees can vary substantially.

Mode of payment:
Understand the different modes of payment that are provided by the exchange. Maybe they use credit cards, debit cards, wire transfers, or even PayPal. If an exchange has restricted or

limited payment options, then it might not be the most convenient option available for you. Whenever you want to purchase any cryptocurrency with your credit card, then you will need to verify your identity, and this also comes with a higher transaction and processing fees. Also, the risk of fraud is higher too. Acquiring cryptocurrency through a wire transfer can take a while since it needs to be processed and verified by the concerned bank first.

Verification:
Most of the trading platforms located in the US and UK require some form of ID proof for making deposits and withdrawals. There are some that provide anonymity. The process of verification can take up to a couple of days, and it might seem a little troublesome. But it is in your interest, and it helps in protecting the exchange from the possibility of theft, fraud, and other scams.

Geographical restrictions:
There are a few user-specific functions like an exchange offer, which is accessible only in certain countries.

Make sure that the exchange you are opting for provides complete access to all tools and functions regardless of the country you are located in.

Exchange rate:
Different exchanges have different exchange rates. You will probably be surprised about the amount that you can save by doing a little bit of research. At times, the exchange rates can go up to 10% or even higher. So, do your research carefully.

Best cryptocurrency exchanges
There are plenty of platforms, and they all aren't created equally. The list of platforms mentioned below includes some of the most popular cryptocurrency exchanges regarding user-friendliness, fees charged, accessibility, and the security offered. Here is the list of the best exchanges in no particular order.

Coinbase:
This is widely trusted by several investors and is used by millions of individuals globally. Coinbase is amongst the most popular crypto

exchanges, famous brokers, and well-known trading platforms in the world at the moment. Coinbase makes it easy for securely buying, using, storing, and trading digitized currency. Users can cryptocurrencies like Bitcoins, Litecoins, and Ethereum by using this website through a digital wallet that is available for devices supported by android and iOS. They can also trade with other users by using the Global Digital Asset Exchange or GDAX subsidiary of Coinbase. GDAX is currently operation in the US, UK, Europe, Canada, Australia, and Singapore. There is no exchange fee that is chargeable by GDAX currently for transferring funder between the Coinbase and GDAX accounts. For now, depending on the country you reside in, the selection of tradable currencies will vary. You can head to their website to learn more about this platform.

This platform has a good reputation, offers security, the transactional cost is reasonable, the interface is user-friendly, and the currency that's stored in Coinbase is covered by its insurance. However, on the flipside, the customer support needs to improve, the payment options are limited, it is available in only a limited number of countries, the rollout of services isn't uniform, and GDAX is apt for technical traders.

Kraken:

It was founded in the year 2011, and it is the largest Bitcoin exchange platform in the euro volume traded and liquidity offered. It is a partner in the first cryptocurrency bank created as well. Kraken allows its users to buy and sell Bitcoins and trade Bitcoins in exchange for euros, US dollars, Canadian dollars, British pounds, and the Japanese yen. The other cryptocurrencies that can be traded on this platform include Ethereum or ether, Monero, Augur REP tokens, Ripple, ICONOMI, Litecoin, Zcash, Dogecoin, and Lumens. For the experienced users, Kraken also offers margin trading other advanced trading features. Check the official website of Kraken for gaining better insight.

This platform boasts of good reputation, reasonable fair exchange rates, the cost of transactions is low, the deposit fee is minimal, offers plenty of features, provides good customer support, very secure, and is supported all over the world. On the downside, the payment options are limited, it is not the best platform for beginners, and the user interface isn't intuitive.

Cex.io:

This platform provides a host of services for the users of Bitcoins and other cryptocurrencies. It allows its users to easily trade their fiat currency for cryptocurrencies and the other way around as well. If you are looking for a platform that will allow the users to trade in Bitcoins professionally, then Cex.io offers several personalized trading dashboards that are user-friendly and provides the option of margin trading as well. Not just that, but it provides novice traders with a really simple way of buying Bitcoins at a price that is almost the same as the market rate. This website is secure, and the cryptocurrencies can be stored in the safe for cold storage.

This platform enjoys a good reputation, it supports credit cards, a good mobile application, and good for beginners, the exchange rates are decent, and it provides worldwide support. However, the customer support is just about average, the process of verification is lengthy, and depositing is quite expensive.

ShapeShift:

This is one of the leading exchanged, and it supports different types of cryptocurrencies like Bitcoin, ether, Monero, Zcash, dash, Dogecoin, and many others as well. This is an excellent option for anyone who is interested in conducting straightforward trades without having to sign up, creating a platform or having to depend on a platform for the safekeeping of their funds. This platform doesn't allow a user to purchase cryptocurrency by making use of credit or debit cards. The platform has a strict no fiat money policy and is solely for the exchange of one cryptocurrency for another cryptocurrency. Please do visit their official website to learn more about their trading policies.

This trading platform has a good reputation in the market, is beginner friendly, the prices are reasonable, the time for processing a transaction is less, and it offers plenty of cryptocurrencies. On the down side, their mobile application isn't that great; it doesn't allow any fiat currencies, the payment options are limited, and provides only a few tools.

Poloniex:
It is one of the most popular cryptocurrency exchanges, and it was founded in the year 2014. The transaction provides a secured trading platform with over 100 Bitcoin-cryptocurrency pairings and several advanced tools and data analysis as well. This trading platform has one of the highest trading volumes recorded, and the users always have the option of closing their trade position. It uses a volume-tiered and a maker-taker schedule for fees for all the trades. So, the fee payable will be different depending on whether you are a maker or a taker. For makers, the fee can range anywhere from 0-0.15% depending on the quantum of trade conducted. Whereas for takers, the fee can range from 0.10-0.25%. There is no fee levied

on withdrawals that go beyond the transaction fee needed by the network. The chat box offered by this platform is one of its unique features, and this allows the user to obtain help about anything related to cryptocurrencies. Any user is allowed to write what they want, and if the comment is inappropriate, then the moderator can take it down. At times it isn't easy to distinguish between good and bad advice, but the chat box is a great tool to increase user engagement.

The creation of an account on this platform isn't time-consuming, there are plenty of useful features, BTC lending is facilitated, the volume of trading is high, easy to use, the trading fee is low, and it has an open API. However, the customer support service is slow, and it doesn't support fiat currencies.

Bitstamp:
This is a European Union Bitcoin marketplace that was created in 2011. This platform is amongst the first-gen Bitcoin exchanges that have managed to develop a loyal customer base for itself. It is a well-known and quite trusted

throughout the Bitcoin community and is a very safe platform. It offers several security features like the two-step authentication procedure and the multi-signature technology for its cryptocurrency wallet and has a cold storage that is fully insured. It offers 24/7 customer support to its users, and the user interface is multilingual. Starting or creating your account is quite easy. Once you have opened a free account and have made a deposit, then the users are free to start trading as soon as they want to.

This platform enjoys a good reputation, provides high-level security to its users, has worldwide availability, the transaction fee is low, and it is best suited for large transactions. It isn't as user-friendly as other platforms, there are only a couple of payment options it offers, and the deposit fee is high.

CoinMama:
This is a veteran broker exchange, and anyone can visit it for buying Bitcoin or Ethereum by making use of credit cards or cash via MoneyGram or the Western Union. This was created for those who

would like to make an instant or a straightforward purchase of digital currency by using the local fiat currency. This service is available to users all over the world, but there are some countries where the users might not be able to access all the functions provided by this website. The user interface is available in several languages like English, German, French, Russian, and Italian as well.

This is a great platform for users, and it enjoys a good reputation. The user interface is good, it offers different payment options, worldwide availability, and the transaction time is relatively good. However, the exchange rates are high; a premium fee is chargeable on credit cards, no Bitcoin selling function and the customer service is just about average.

Bitsquare:
This is an easy-to-use and user-friendly peer-to-peer exchange that allows the users to buy and sell their Bitcoins in exchange for other cryptocurrencies or even fiat currencies. It markets itself a decentralized peer-to-peer platform and

is accessible instantly and doesn't need any registration and indeed doesn't depend on a central authority. This platform never holds onto the funds of the user expect the trading partners who an exchange their data. The platform provides good security coupled with MultiSigna addresses, a security deposit, and a self-built arbitration system for solving any trading disputes. If anonymity is a high priority for you, then this is a wonderful platform for you.

It enjoys an excellent reputation in the market; it is quite secure and private, a lot of cryptocurrency options are available, it doesn't require the user to sign up for it, it is an open source with worldwide availability, and is best suited for advanced traders. But the payment options offered are limited, the customer support can be better, and it isn't the best place for first-time traders.

LocalBitcoin:
This is a peer-to-peer Bitcoin exchange, and the buyers and sellers are located all over the world. By using this platform, you have the option of meeting up with

others in your surroundings for trading in Bitcoins for cash, sending money through PayPal, Skrill, or Dwolla, or even arrange for the required amount to be deposited at a bank branch. The commission chargeable from sellers is 1%, and the sellers are allowed to set their exchange rates. For making sure that the trade is secure, this platform takes plenty of precautions. This platform always rates the traders transacting on it, and this information is public. Also, whenever a trade is requested, then this platform holds those funds in its escrow account and only when the seller confirms the trade will these funds be released. If something goes wrong, it has its team for resolution of conflicts and disputes between sellers and buyers.

This platform doesn't need an ID, it is user and beginner friendly, it usually is free, the transfers are instant, and it is available all over the world. However, the exchange rates are high, and it doesn't facilitate large purchases of Bitcoins.

Gemini:

This platform was co-founded by Tyler Winklevoss and Cameron Winklevoss. It is a fully regulated and licensed US exchange of Bitcoin and ether. This means that the capital requirements, as well as its regulatory standards, should be similar to a bank. Also, if a deposit is made in US dollars then the same would be held in a bank insured by FDIC and most of the digital currency held on it is in cold storage. It trades in only three currencies, and these are US dollar, Bitcoin, and Ethereum. It doesn't serve any other form of crypto or fiat currencies. The exchange has a maker-taker fee schedule with discounts for a trade of high volume. There is no charge on all the deposits and withdrawals. It is entirely available to its customers in 42 US states, Canada, Hong Kong, Japan, Singapore, South Korea and the UK.

The security and compliance offered are exceptional, it is minimalistic and elegant in its design, is user-friendly, provides excellent analytics, and ensures high liquidity. However, the number of currencies offered is limited, has a small community, doesn't have worldwide availability, and doesn't offer margin trading.

If you are thinking about making your first trade, then make sure that you have plenty of research about the trading platform you are opting for.

Conclusion

I would like to thank you once again for purchasing this book. I hope it proved to be an informative read.

Cryptocurrencies are a wonderful invention and, within a short span of time, they have managed to revolutionize the entire financial system of different economies. By now you will have realized that investing in cryptocurrencies is beneficial and all the benefits they provide the holder with. Make use of the information provided in this book for making your trade without having to rely on any guesswork. It takes a while to get the hang of this new technology, but the returns will undoubtedly make it worth your while. Move over stocks and real estate, the future of investing lies in cryptocurrencies.

Now that you are armed with all the information you have been provided with in this book, you are ready to step into the world of cryptocurrencies. Invest wisely, and you will be able to increase your wealth! Thank you and all the best!

And finally, if you liked the book, I would like to ask you to do me a favor and leave a review for the book on Amazon.

www.ingramcontent.com/pod-product-compliance
Lightning Source LLC
Chambersburg PA
CBHW050105230526
45470CB00004B/1682